ORKNEY

A CELEBRATION OF LIGHT AND LANDSCAPE

Printed by The Orcadian (Kirkwall Press)
Hell's Half Acre, Hatston, Kirkwall, Orkney, Scotland, KW15 1DW
Tel. 01856 879000
www.orcadian.co.uk

Photographs © Iain Sarjeant
www.iainsarjeant.com

Poems © Pam Beasant

ISBN 978-1-902957-39-5

Printed by The Orcadian, Hatston Print Centre,
Hell's Half Acre, Kirkwall, Orkney, Scotland, KW15 1DW

CONTENTS

Hoy from Marwick

INTRODUCTION

Over the years I have tried to capture images which reflect the essence of the Orkney magic which seems to draw me to these islands. They represent a very personal relationship with the place.

I first visited Orkney as a small boy and have returned frequently. Ever since my first visit, I have been deeply moved by the place, and find it an incredibly inspiring group of islands. But putting into words instead of images exactly what makes these islands so special is much harder for me.

It's a heady mix - firstly nowhere have I felt such a sense of the past embedded in the landscape, a history you can feel and touch. This together with what has to be some of the most dramatic coastal landscapes in Scotland, makes Orkney a photographer's dream. But it's more than that, it's also a deeply inspiring place, a friendly vibrant community with a strong creative tradition which rubs off on anyone visiting. Most of all though, Orkney has an incredible quality of light - something truly magical.

I hope you enjoy these photographs and they help create an atmosphere of the Orkney that you know and love too.

Iain Sarjeant
March, 2010

Knap of Howar,
Papa Westray

FOREWORD

From the early days of photography in the late 1800s when top hats, glass slides and eternal patience were absolute requirements for button men, to the digital era with its instantaneous avalanche of pix, the green isles of Orkney have always been a popular subject for the camera lens. This splendid new photographic collection from Ross-shire based Iain Sarjeant, enriched by the poems of our own Pam Beasant, will be a treasure for all who love Orkney. It is a genuine challenge for Iain to follow in the footsteps of now legendary figures like Tom Kent, Willie Hourston and Gunnie Moberg and at a time when Orkney has a new batch of generally young and talented photographers. However, this book emerges as a truly sensuous experience with a string of memorable images from a mist-shrouded Brodgar to the wild tidelines of my home isle, Papa Westray. In the daily newspaper business I was always suspicious of photographers casually pressing a button and producing wonderful, occasionally timeless, images while the poor hack struggled endlessly over a scatter of mere words. Photography seemed to me almost like a dark art. As the book title suggests light embraces the Orkney landscape in an almost spiritual manner. And in these pages Iain has somehow captured that coming together. If that isn't magic, I don't know what is.

Jim Hewitson
Papa Westray
February, 2010

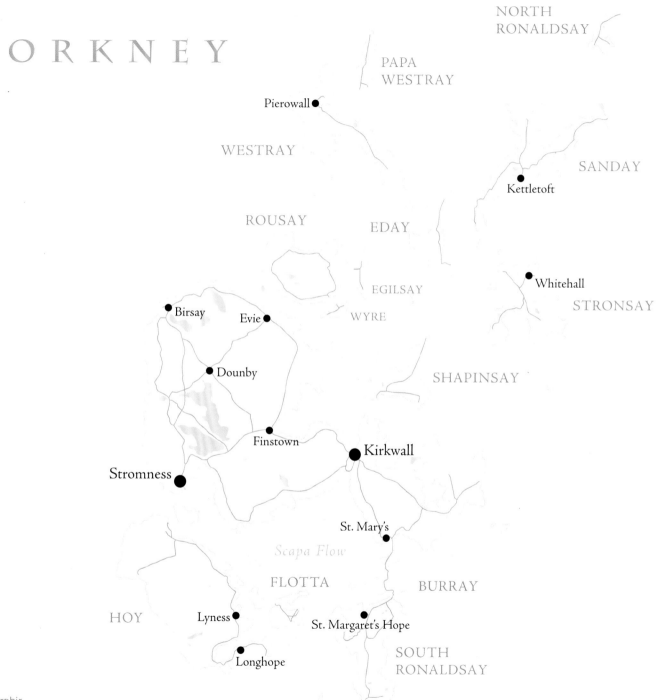

ORKNEY

NORTH
RONALDSAY

PAPA
WESTRAY

Pierowall●

WESTRAY

SANDAY

Kettletoft●

ROUSAY

EDAY

EGILSAY

●Birsay   Evie●

WYRE

Whitehall●

STRONSAY

●Dounby

SHAPINSAY

Finstown●

●Kirkwall

Stromness●

St. Mary's●

Scapa Flow

FLOTTA

BURRAY

HOY   Lyness●

St. Margaret's Hope●

●Longhope

SOUTH
RONALDSAY

Farmland near Orphir

Carved stone in St. Magnus Cathedral, Kirkwall

PART I ECHOES OF THE PAST

The Ring of Brodgar at dawn

The Ring of Brodgar at sunrise

The Ring of Brodgar

The Ring of Brodgar at sunrise

The Stones of Stenness
at sunset

The Stones of Stenness

This place

Sky hurls down from everywhere
pushing low curves flatter.
They are sculpted gradually
by weather-lapping.

It's an odd beauty
expressed in the cracked lilt of the voices
and sweeping farms that accommodate
trows and standing stones.

Faces here are set to scale
in space and time,
history frames them.
The city cult of the self is abashed.

Incomers, always aliens,
embrace life; look over its shoulder,
wide-eyed, as it proclaims itself
loudly in sandstone and rune.

The Ring of Brodgar

Skara Brae

Knap of Howar, Papa Westray

Midhowe Cairn, Rousay

Out of time

Time moves, feline, on a pliable curve;
sometimes it sleeps, then paces warily,
sometimes it runs, full-stretch.

A face slips into focus,
from nowhere, after all these years.

Time, the big cat on the monumental track,
runs either way, goes on and back;
pounces, just occasionally.
We step sideways, heart-stopped.

The Unstan Cairn and
Loch of Stenness at dawn

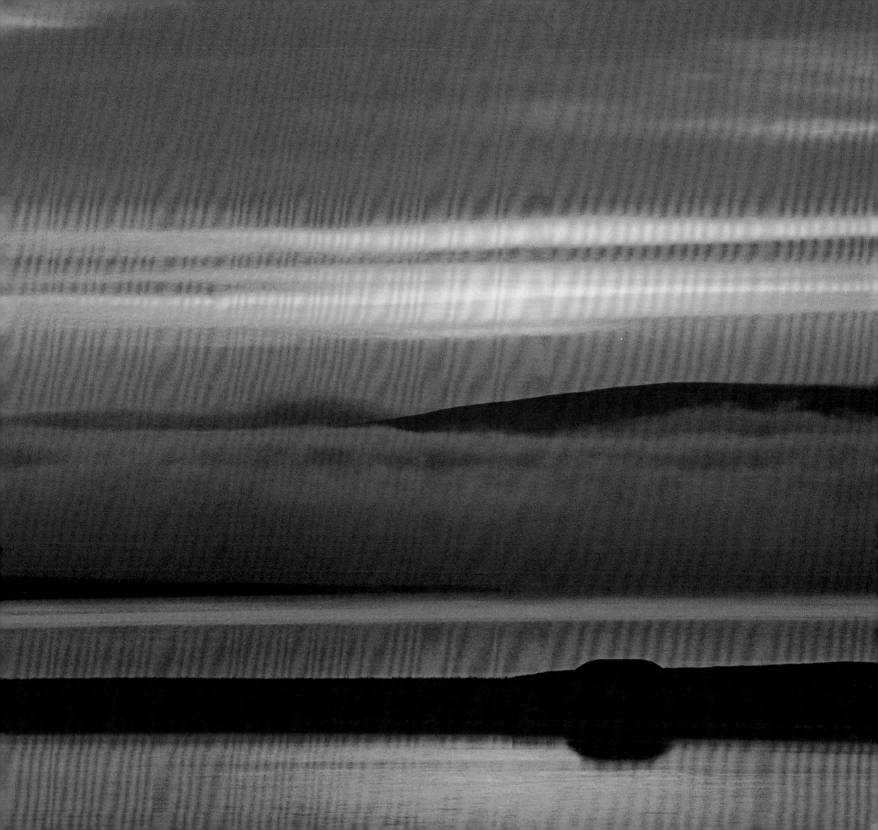

Wideford Hill Cairn, near Kirkwall

Knap of Howar, Papa Westray

21

Burroughston Broch, Shapinsay

The Broch of Gurness

St. Magnus Cathedral,
Kirkwall

Doorway detail, St. Magnus Cathedral, Kirkwall

Kirbuster Farm Museum

29

The Birsay Whalebone

In praise of the sun

It blocks out night, the galaxy,
space yawning to infinity
(if that's what it does),
the idea bending the mind
with improbability.
Better to get down on bended knee,
give thanks to the big obstacle
that puts time and order
between us and an endless mad gap.

Hoxa Head, South Ronaldsay

WW2 signal station, Stanger Head, Flotta

Flotta

The Italian Chapel, Lamb Holm

34

The Italian Chapel,
Lamb Holm

Breaking waves, Birsay

PART 2   A MEETING OF OCEANS

Warebeth beach in the evening, near Stromness

Yesnaby at sunset

Postcard from Hoy

Storm threatens on Ward Hill
overflowing the valley's bowl
but holds, leaving Rackwick yolk-lit, eerie,
its colours against deep grey
bold as a fable.

A seal leaves marks in the sand
escaping voices, feet, intruders,
skin rippled with muscle-alarm.
Its head bobs, sleek-metallic,
watching from the safety of the undertow.

Up the cliff path, they crocodile,
kitted out for dire emergency,
passing a perilous drop to the wrinkled sea.
It invites. Jump. You'll barely make a dent.
Hearts falter, bare legs tremble a little.

Thunder between the hills still holds,
not relieving shimmering air.
They snap, take home
a picture of something longed for,
a perfect silence, achieved.

The Old Man of Ho

The Old Man of Hoy
at sunset

Yesnaby Castle
at sunset

Costa Head, near Evie

The Vat O' Kirbister,
Stronsay

Groattie buckie hunt

There's a couple lying on the grassy slope
above the pebbles, not touching
but intimate, splayed out,
wind coming straight off the sea,
flattening them.

After that – no one.
Just rocks in jagged, joined formation,
mini-cliffs, and green slime
round stagnant pools,
clusters of shells and stones that look promising.

But no. Legs ache bending
up and down in the search,
poking a stick through shingle,
moving on.
I might be the last one left alive.

Then, plump brown-spotted,
tight-lipped groatties
give themselves up
and, rounding a rocky corner
on a ledge, to keep feet

Dingieshowe,
Deerness

out of the sea, the Black Craig
rises in the foreground like an ancient
warning, shockingly close,
looming over flesh and bone.
Suddenly,

a baby cormorant moves
underfoot,
as startled as me,
hot-pads it to a crevice,
disappears.

Run back, from rock to stone to shingle, sand,
the glimpse of the car park
far round the shore.
Later, ankles aching on the sofa
counting the prizes

cleaning them of grit and beach
holding them on the flat of a hot hand.

Mull Head, Deerness

Marwick Head at sunset

Noup Head,
Westray

Noup Hea
Westra

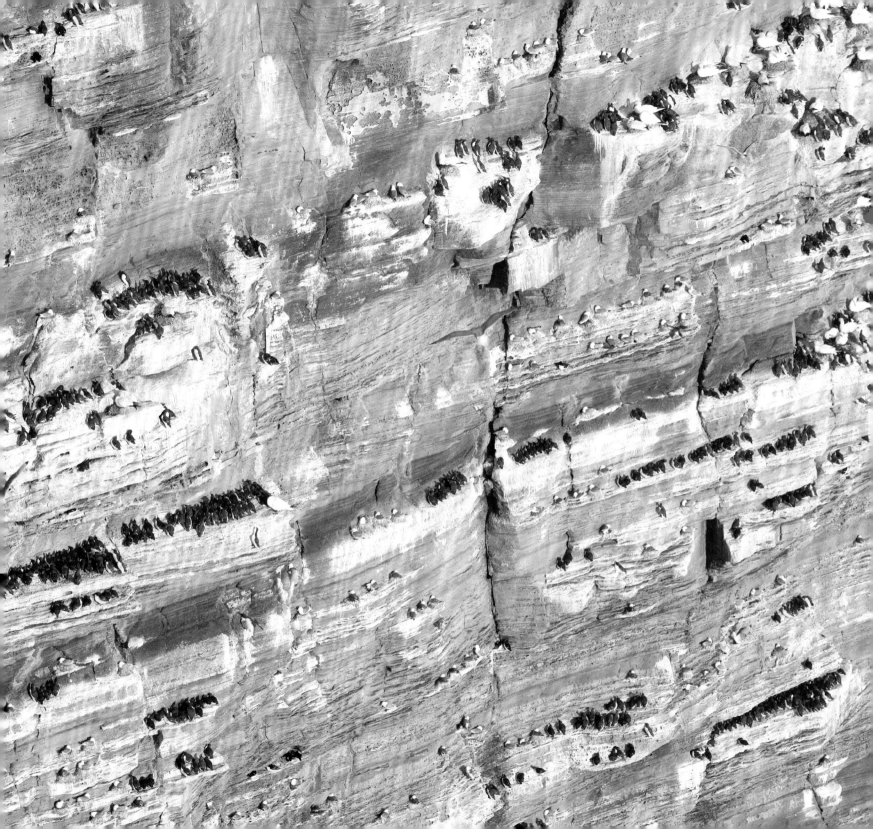

Puffin resting, Fowl Craig, Papa Westray

Puffins, Fowl Craig, Papa Westray

Rackwick Bay, Hoy

Kelp, South Ronaldsay

Sand of Mussetter,
Eday

Sunset from the we[st]
coast of Papa Westr[ay]

Dingieshowe, Deerness

58

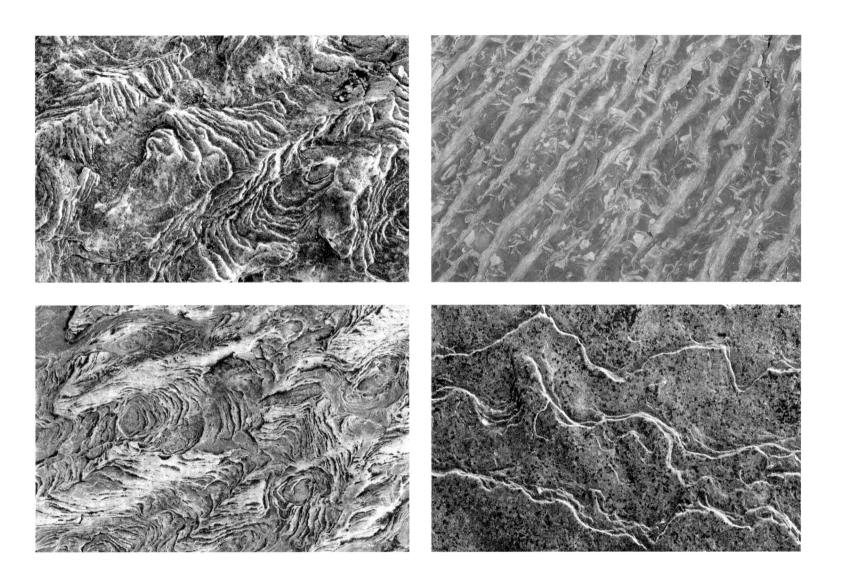

Hoy from Warebeth

Marwick Head at sunset

The Brough of Birsay

The tide draws back at bay,
emerging causeway
glimpses then connects the island, only half astray.

Slipping in pools, picking over seaweed,
avoiding fulmars that vomit to protect their eggs
we edge towards it.

Bodiless seals bob
watching clumsy rubber feet
going tentative from land to land.

Young Magnus, loved by seals,
grew tall and half-tame there in the monks' school.
(Culled on Egilsay, his skull lies bricked up,
dry in his cathedral.)

The brough guards ghosts, ruins
tended by the elements -
rain comes in to hose the grass,
wind-raked, polished by the sun,
and we, sea-conquerors, approach.

Stay until the causeway drowns,
fulmars wheel away.
Spooked by sudden silence,
we wade back, stumbling;
seal eyes wide at our backs.

Birsay
causeway

At Skaill

I want to watch you
in golden light
at Skaill, water
mercury,
spilling the tide
cross-ways,
horizon broken peaks.

I want to watch the light
pick out gold in your hair.
I want to watch you like this
forever, at Skaill.

Kelp, Burray

64

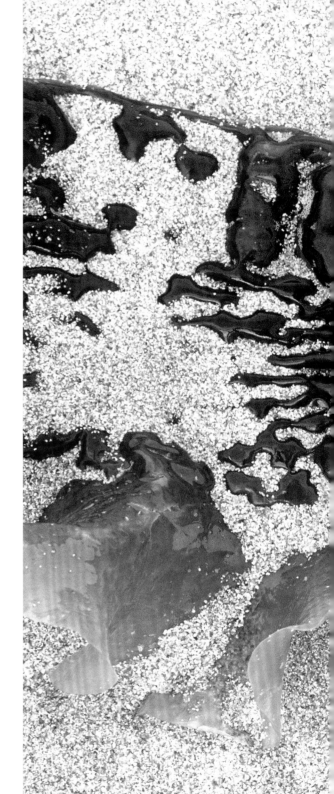

Sunset from Sands of Mussetter, Eday

North Wick, Papa Westray

Grobust,
Westray

The origin of the theorem

Peeling slime off his sodden sandal
Pythagoras stares excited at the wet triangle
he stepped in.

Wiggling his toes in salty ozone
he scribbles calculations on the sandstone
muttering to no one
then squelches back to the inn.

Who'd have thought that nature could be
so mathematical in Westray? -
he muses later, in the bath,
displacing water complacently.

He knows his eureka moment
is just as good as Archimedes'.

In fact, whichever angle you take,
it all adds up.

Burray

Seaweed patter
Whitehall, Strons

Rousay from Evie

Graemsay and Hoy from Stenness

Morning mist over Graemsay and Hoy

Grobust, Westray

Sea Rocket, Stronsay

The Old Man of Hoy
at sunset

Sunset over Bay of Ireland

Stromness

PART 3 ISLAND LIFE

Stromness

Harbour reflections, Stromness

Stromness reflections

Stromness

The new Pierhead

The creels, like an art installation,
will go, and corrugated roofs
will be replaced by wood
and sympathetic stone
and the pierhead will be proud,
well-designed,
but the lovely creels will go.
And this is good,
but, like the days when you could walk
across the harbour, boat to boat,
and no one thought of how it looked
too busy working raw hands
glad to have made the shelter of the town.
Like these days, the creels will go.

Kirkwall

Kirkwall

Black Guillemot (or Tystie), Whitehall village, Stronsay

Old boat, Westray

Westray

Hoy from Orkney Mainland

Keats' field

Graphic lines of fertile gold
proclaim
beauty is food; food beauty.

Feed us with beauty
until we are golden dust
feeding food.

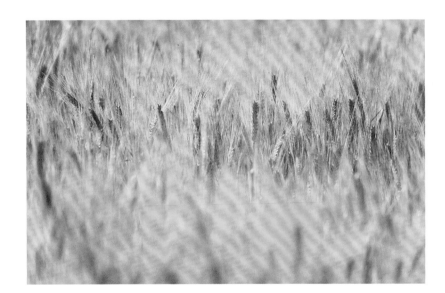

Farmland
near Yesnaby

95

Rinansay

Sheep and kirk,
croft and lighthouse,
wreck on treacherous reef;
green, gold, grey,
crumbling stone, lichen-
covered – every inch
could have been touched
by hand, hoof or gull's
stick leg. Dig and dig,
find new meaning in
layers of soil, of
genealogy.
Re-invent
this subtle, parallel
place, that makes north
true, possible, outlined,
like a ghost's drawn breath.

North Ronaldsay
sheep

e dry stone dyke,
rth Ronaldsay

97

nland
Yesnaby

Start Point,
Sanday

St. Margaret's Hope, South Ronaldsay

Pierowall, Westray

Kirkwall

Stromness

Ruined cottage overlooking Fersness Bay, Eday

Calfsound, Eday

Looking across to Rousay from Evie

Sunset near Orphir

Haiku

Red ribbon of sunset
dissolves into
particles of woven dark.

ACKNOWLEDGEMENTS

I am honoured to have poems by Pam Beasant laced through the pages of this book, wonderful words which evoke such feeling. Thank you Pam!

Many people helped and supported me over the years in being able to take these images and produce this book, too many to name. But a special thanks goes to my wife Iona and my boys Andrew and Calum for giving me the time to disappear and endulge myself in my passion. These images would not have been possible without them. Also my thanks to Duncan and Marlene Finlayson for every year providing us with such a wonderful home from home.

For fine hospitality and a bed for the night on Hoy, many thanks to Charlie Bateman. Thanks also to Jennifer Foley for being so accommodating on Papa Westray.

Many thanks to Jim Hewitson for writing such a wonderful foreword to this book, and also for his and Morag's warm hospitality on Papa Westray - possibly the tastiest meal I've had in Orkney!

Thanks to James Miller at the Orcadian for taking the project on, and Drew Kennedy for all his help and advice with the preparation of the book.

Finally a thank you to all who've stopped and blethered with me along the way, I value every connection!